Contents

Fish and Chips
and Other Adventures

David Couper

MACMILLAN
PUBLISHERS

First published 1991

Published by
MACMILLAN PUBLISHERS LIMITED
London and Basingstoke

Cover design and illustration by Indent, Reading

Illustrated by Peter Kent

Typeset by Macmillan Production Limited

Printed in Singapore

A CIP catalogue record for this book is available from
the British Library

ISBN 0-333-51258-8

Introduction

Jim lives with his family in the north of England. They like living there, but now life is not very easy because Jim has no job, and there is not a lot of work in the town. What can you do when your family is hungry, but you have no work and no money?

Well, Jim is not a man to sit down and feel sorry for himself. He goes off to find work in London in the south of England, and then he tries to start his own business. We follow Jim's story as he tries one idea after another to make money—and Jim has some very strange ideas! Something always seems to go wrong . . . Is everything going to be OK in the end?

Jim worked in a factory in the north of England. One day, the factory closed and he lost his job. He did not have any money, but he still had a hungry family. His friend Tom was lucky. He had a supermarket. It was very busy. Everybody bought food there.

~ ∎ ~

One day in the pub, Jim and Tom talked.
    'What am I going to do?' Jim said.
    'I don't know. You haven't got a job and you haven't got any money. You need a new job.'
    'Yes, I know. I'm not stupid. But there isn't any work here; there are no jobs for anyone.'
    'That's true. Everybody here wants a job.'
    'Have you got any jobs in your supermarket?'
    'No, I'm sorry, I haven't . . . Here, have another beer.'
    He didn't know what to do, so he drank another beer. Then Tom bought another one and after that they smiled: life was not so bad.

There was a television in the pub and they watched the news.

'I can't listen. It's terrible.'
'No jobs, no work. It's terrible.'
They drank some beer and then they drank some more.
'It's terrible, terrible. Really terrible.'

'What can I do?'
'I don't know.'
Then suddenly Tom smiled. 'I know.'
'What?' Jim shouted.
'Go to London. Yes, go to the south. Get a job there.'
'But I don't *like* London.'
'But you – '
'No.'

~ ■ ~

At home, Polly, Jim's wife, was crying.

'Don't cry, Polly.'

'We don't have any money.'

'I know. But Tom says it's better in the south.'

'What?' she said.

He showed her the newspaper. 'Look at these jobs, they're all in the south.'

'I don't like the south,' Polly said. 'It's too busy. In the north there aren't too many people, and there's more countryside.'

'Yes, London *is* busy. It has too many cars and people. But listen, Polly, there aren't any jobs.'

'I'm not going to London. I love the north, our town, the family and you.'

He kissed her. 'But I need money and a job.'

'I know. I know. You're right.' She kissed him too. 'But I'm going to stay here.'

'Yes, OK. You stay in the house with the kids.'

~ ■ ~

The next day, he went south. He got a train. All his family were at the station. He had his suitcase and some food. Polly had got him some fish and chips. He loved fish and chips. His son, Simon, gave him his favourite toy car and Suzie, his daughter, gave him her radio. He would be able to listen to the news and to music in London.

'Goodbye,' he said to them.
'Bye,' they all shouted. Polly was crying, but Jim still got on the train.
Inside the train, he looked at his ticket. It was the wrong ticket. It was not a ticket to London.

~ ■ ~

At the station, Polly got on another train. She was going to take the children to a big house called Bigwig Castle. It was a very nice place. They were going to visit the house and walk in the gardens. But when she looked at her ticket, it was to London. She screamed and everyone looked at her. She put her head out of the window
and saw Jim.
'I have your ticket!' she shouted.
'What?'
'*I've got your ticket!*'
But it was no good because the two
trains were going different ways.

Jim shut the window and sat down. The guard stopped in front of him.
'Ticket, please.'

'Yes. You want my ticket. Just a moment, please.' Jim was frightened. He looked at the ticket that he held in his hand.

'Ticket, sir, please.'

'I don't have a ticket.'

'What, no ticket?'

'No. My wife has my ticket. I have a ticket to Bigwig Castle.'

'To Bigwig Castle? This train doesn't go to Bigwig Castle.'

'I know, but – '

'Sorry, sir, you need a ticket. Get off at the next station.'

'But I'm going to London.'

'You don't have the right train ticket, sir. You need a ticket to London, not a ticket to Bigwig Castle.'

'But – '

'OK. You can buy a ticket: I sell tickets.'

'Oh, all right. Give me a ticket, please.'

'Right, sir. Here you are. That's sixty-five pounds, please.'

'*How* much?'

'Sixty-five pounds. A ticket to London.'

'But I don't have enough money.'

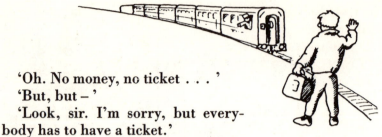

'Oh. No money, no ticket . . . '
'But, but – '
'Look, sir. I'm sorry, but every-
body has to have a ticket.'
The train stopped and Jim got off.
'Goodbye,' said the guard.

~ ■ ~

The station was empty. Polly was not there. He rang her,
but she wasn't at home. He sat and waited. Then he rang
her again.
'Polly?'
'Yes, Jim? Where are you?'
'At Newtown station.'
'Newtown station?'
'Yes. I've got the wrong ticket, so I got off the train. I
need the ticket to London and you've got that.'
'Yes, dear. I'm sorry. I wanted to go to Bigwig Castle
with the children.'
'Well, come to the station, Polly, and bring my ticket,
and then I can go to London.'
'Yes, dear. Right, dear. Sorry, dear.'
He waited at the station, ten minutes, twenty minutes,
half an hour . . . He was angry and it was cold. Finally,
Polly arrived.
'Here's your ticket, dear, and here's some more fish and
chips.'
'Thanks, and here's yours. The next train is going in
twenty minutes.'
'Oh well, goodbye.' She kissed him and cried a little.
'Goodbye.'

~ ■ ~

The train arrived and Jim got on.
  He sat down and fell asleep.
  The guard came.
  'Tickets, please.'
  Jim was asleep.
  '*Tickets*.'
  Jim was still asleep.
  'Tickets! Wake up!' the guard shouted.
  'What? What? Yes, dear.'

But it was not Polly: it was the guard.
  'Tickets.'
  It was the same guard.
  'Here you are. I've got it now.'
  'Good. Ah. Sorry, but this is the
wrong ticket.'
  'What do you mean? It's the
right ticket!'
  'No, it isn't. This ticket is
to London.'

  'Yes, I know. I'm going to London. I need work and
there are lots of jobs in London.'
  'Yes, I know,' the guard said. 'But this train is going to
Scotland. It's going north, not south.'
  'Oh no. This is the wrong train. The right ticket but the
wrong train.'
  'You must get off, sir.'
  'Right.'

~ ■ ~

Poor Jim got off and waited for the next train. He got on and slept; he was very tired. He got off in London and it was late evening. He found a hotel and slept.

In the morning he got up and then had breakfast in a small, dirty cafe.

'What do you want?' said the waitress.

'Eggs and tea, please.'

'Right. Do you want anything else?'

'No, no thanks. Only a job.'

'A job? Well, there's a factory near here. Ask Mr Jones; he's the boss.'

'Thank you.'

He went to the factory. He saw a door. It was Mr Jones's office. He knocked on the door.

'Come in,' Mr Jones shouted. He was sitting at a big desk and he was reading a newspaper.

'Hello. My name is Jim Giles.'

'Oh yes, and what do you want?' He was still reading his newspaper.

'I want a job, please.'

'OK, what do you do?'

'Well, I do anything. In the north, I worked in a factory.'

'I don't have any jobs. There's no work here. I'm sorry.'

Jim was very sad.

'Go to Bert Ragley. He's a friend. He has a shop.'

'Oh, does he have jobs?'

'Sometimes.'

'Thank you. Thank you very much, Mr Jones.'

But Mr Jones did not say anything. He just read his newspaper.

Jim went to the shop. It was a big shop and it was very busy.

'Hello. Is Mr Ragley here?'

'Yes, and who are you?' asked a woman.

'Oh, my name's Jim. Jim Giles.'

'What do you want?'

'I want a job.'

The woman laughed. 'Everybody wants a job. Mr Ragley is very busy, he doesn't talk to everybody.'

'Oh. But he has a friend called Mr Jones. He has a factory.'

'Are you a friend of Mr Jones?'

'Well, I know him.'

'Oh, well. Then come in.'

He went into a big office. Mr Ragley was asleep.
'What? Who are you?'

'I'm Jim Giles. Mr Jones – '
'Oh, Percy Jones. He's a good friend . . . What do you want?'
'I want a job.'
'Oh, I'm sorry. We don't have any jobs. Next year, I'm going to need somebody.'
'But – '
'Sorry, no. Thank you, thank you.'
Jim was very, very sad. The next day he ate breakfast. The waitress smiled.
'How are you today?'
'OK.'
'Have you got a job?'
'No, there are no jobs at the factory and no jobs at the shop.'
'Oh dear. Can you cook?'
'Well, yes. I can.'
'Good. We need a cook.'

'What, you need a cook here?
Here in the restaurant?'
'Yes, that's right.'
'Oh great.'
'Good! Start tomorrow.'
Jim was so happy. He had a job.
The money was not very good, but
it was still a job.

~ ∎ ~

The kitchen was very hot. He cooked breakfast and then he
cooked more food. He was very tired. The customers were
very difficult. One man only liked burnt toast. Another lady
liked a lot of milk in her coffee. One girl always had two eggs
and no bacon. Sometimes he made mistakes.

One day, the guard came in and saw Jim in the kitchen.

'Oh, it's you. You work here. I want coffee and toast,
and no butter.'

Jim was very busy in the kitchen. He gave the waitress
tea and toast with butter and jam. The guard was angry.

'This isn't right. You always get it wrong. I said coffee
and toast, *no butter*.'

Jim made more toast.

Every day was the same. He never sat down and he was
really tired.

~ ∎ ~

He phoned Polly.
   'Hello, it's me.'
   'Who?'
   'Jim. Jim, your husband.'
   'Oh, sorry, dear. How are you?'
   'Fine. I've got a job.'
   'Great, what are you doing?'
   'I work in a kitchen.'
   'In a kitchen?'
   'Yes, I'm a cook.'
   'Oh. Is the money good?'
   'No, but it's a job.'
   'Yes, dear. Oh well.'
   'Yes. I'm going to work now. Bye.'
   'Bye.'

~ ■ ~

He worked in the kitchen for three weeks. The work was very, very hard and he was always tired.
   He called Polly again.

   'Hello. How's work?' she said.
   'Work? Work's hard. I'm so tired.'
   'Oh dear. Come home.'
   'I like home. I don't like London.'
   '*Come home*.'
   'But I need a job and money.'
   'But we need you, so come home. Come home tomorrow.

~ ■ ~

He went home. Polly and the children were very happy.

'But I still need a job,' he said.

He ate his dinner of fish and chips.

'My favourite food,' he said.

'I know, dear.'

'Where do you buy fish and chips?'

'Well, there isn't a fish and chip
shop nearby.'

'Oh. So where do you go?'

'I go to Newtown.'

'But Newtown isn't nearby. You
have to get a bus.'

'Yes, I know. But you like fish and
chips.'

'They're delicious.'

Later, in bed, while his wife was
asleep, he was thinking.

'Fish and chips!' he shouted.

'What?' She woke up. 'Fish and chips?'

'Fish and chips is the answer!'

'Answer?'

'Yes. I need a job, and fish and chips is going to be my new job.'

'I don't understand.'

'I'm going to buy a van and I'm going to sell fish and chips.'

'I still don't understand.'

'I'm going to sell fish and chips in our town. And I'm going to sell fish and chips in towns nearby.'

'I don't understand.'

'There is no fish and chip shop nearby, so I'm going to – '

'Oh, you're going to buy a shop, and sell fish and chips in our town.'

'No, I'm not going to buy a shop. I'm going to buy a van.'

'A van?'

'Yes. People buy ice-cream from a van. Well, I'm going to sell fish and chips from a van.'

'So you're going to sell fish and chips from a van. That's stupid.'

'No, it isn't.'

'I'm going to be rich.'

'Go to sleep.'

~ ■ ~

But Jim didn't have any money. He couldn't buy a van because he needed money.

Luckily, Tom had money. His supermarket was very busy.
Jim saw Tom in the pub.

'Tom, I'm back.'

'No jobs in the south?'

'No good jobs. But I've got a good idea for a business.'

'Great. Do you want another beer?'

'Thanks. Tom, I need some money.'

'I don't understand.'

'I need some money for my idea.'

'How much?'

'One thousand pounds.'

'One thousand pounds is a lot of money.'

'But it's a good idea.'

'What's the idea?'

'Well, I want a van and then I can sell fish and chips in our town and in the other towns nearby.'

'That's stupid.'

'No, it isn't. I only need a van.'

'Vans are expensive. This is a stupid idea.'

'No, it's not.'

'How about a bicycle?'

'A bicycle? I need a van, not a bicycle. That's a stupid idea.'

'Bicycles are cheap – only about fifty pounds.'

'Are you going to lend me fifty pounds?'

'Yes, fifty pounds isn't too much money. A cheap idea is the best one.'

'OK, OK. Thank you. I'm going to buy a bicycle and then next year I'm going to buy a van.'

'Right! This year you sell fish and chips in our town only. Next year you sell fish and chips in the nearby towns too.'

'Good. Are you going to give me the money now?'

'OK. There you are: fifty pounds.'

The next day Jim bought a bicycle. He got a bicycle with a big basket. It was not a new one, but it was a good one.

Polly went to the fish shop and bought some fish.

'Good morning, Mrs Giles.'

'Good morning. I need some fish. Fifty-five pieces of fish.'

'Fifty-five pieces of fish?

'Yes, fifty-five pieces of fish. We're going to have a fish and chip shop.'

'Oh, I see.'

Simon, their son, bought lots of potatoes.

'Hi, Simon!' said Simon's friend, Tony.

'I want some potatoes, Tony. Five sacks.'

'Five sacks? Are you going to sell
fish and chips?' he laughed.

'Yes, we are. Bye.'

At home, Jim was hungry.

'What are we going to eat for dinner?' he said. 'I'd like a
steak.'

'We're going to have fish.'

The next day, he went on his bicycle with his fish and
chips. No-one bought any fish and chips. He didn't understand. His fish and chips were wonderful. Everyone knew
that. And they were cheap. He tried and tried, but he did
not sell any. All his fish and chips got cold. He went home
and told Polly.

'What! But that's stupid. You're lazy and no good. I'm
going to sell some.'

So she got on the bicycle and took some hot fish and
chips with her.

She talked to a woman in the street.

'Would you like some, dear? They're really nice. I cook
them myself.'

'How much are they?'

'One pound fifty.'

'Oh, no. I can get them much cheaper.'

'Where?' Polly was really surprised.

'At Wonder-Eats. The shop on the High Street.'

'Oh. Thanks, dear.'

Polly rode off. She cycled very fast and some of the fish and chips fell off, but she didn't stop. She wanted to find out about Wonder-Eats.

In the High Street, there was a big queue of about fifty people outside Wonder-Eats. She could not believe it. She stopped outside and looked in. The shop sold fish and chips and burgers. There was a big notice which said: 'Special Price – Fish and Chips £1.00.' There was a tall, thin man standing behind the counter. He smiled when he saw her.

'Your business isn't doing very well, is it?' He laughed loudly and then started coughing. He had a cigarette in his hand. 'You had better start something different.' He laughed loudly again. 'Like a bicycle shop. You have one bike already.'

All the customers looked round and laughed. Polly was really angry and she rode home very fast. All the fish and chips fell off the bike. But she didn't stop.

When she got home, she started crying.

'I'm so angry. It's not fair. That man is horrible. He took away our business. He's just greedy and selfish.'

'Don't worry. I'll think of something,' Jim said.

They went to bed, and the next day Jim saw Tom in the pub. He explained about the problem.

'It's easy. You have to do better food at a cheaper price,' Tom said.

'Cheaper?'

'Yes, make the food cheaper. Fish and chips for eighty pence. And have burgers and chicken and – I don't know – jacket potatoes.'

'So we fight him?'

'Yes.'

Jim told Polly and she was excited.

'Right, I'll buy some chicken and potatoes and burgers and cook them. And also we should sell drinks: lemonade, cola and beer.'

'That's a great idea.'

Jim cycled off.

At the first house, a woman bought some chicken and chips.

'Delicious,' said the woman.

'This is a great idea,' said a little boy. He ate a burger. 'I love fish and chips. Give me some for my family and some lemonade.'

Jim went back to the house and they cooked some more fish and chips. All day, he sold fish and chips, chicken, baked potatoes and burgers. Everyone wanted to buy the delicious food. They took a lot of money.

The next day, Polly bought a lot of food: chicken, fish, potatoes, burgers, and ketchup, vinegar and salt, as well as bottles of cola, orange and beer. But when she took some to the first house, she was surprised.

'No, thank you,' said the woman. 'You're too expensive.'

Polly rode to the shop in the High Street. The owner was standing outside. He had lots of customers and was very happy. His prices were even lower. Polly could not believe it.

'What are we going to do? We can't fight him. His prices are too low now,' she told Jim.

'He's won.'

'But what are we going to do with all the food?'

She looked at her kitchen. It was full of boxes and crates.

Polly was really angry and Jim was upset. His business was a failure.

'What are we going to do with all this food?' she shouted again.

'I don't know.' Then he sat down.

'I'm going to make some tea,' Polly said.

'OK.'

He sat and thought about the food. The whole kitchen was full of boxes and crates.

'We can *eat* the fish and the chicken.'

'What?' Polly brought the tea in. 'You're stupid. We can put the fish and the chicken in the freezer in Tom's supermarket, but we're going to sell them. I can't eat them.'

'All right.' He drank some tea. 'I know. We can have a new business. We can sell food.'

'OK, OK. But I don't want all this food in my kitchen.'

~ ■ ~

The next day, he went to a hotel.

'Hello. Can I see the cook, please?'

'Why? She's busy now. It's breakfast,' the hotel manager said.

'I sell food: fish and chicken. It's very cheap.'

'Why? Is it stolen?'

'No, no. I bought too much. It's a special price.'

'No. No, thanks.' And the manager shut the door.

MANAGER

The next hotel was the same, and the next one, and the next one. No-one wanted to buy frozen fish or chicken. Then he went to a small hotel. He rang the doorbell and a man in white with a chef's hat opened it.

'Yes?' he shouted. He had a bowl in his hand and he looked very hot.

'I'm sorry, are you busy?'
'Yes, of course I am. I'm cooking lunch.'
'I sell fish and chicken.'
'Sell *fish*?'
Jim looked sad. His new business was no good.
'That's great,' the man said, smiling. He looked really happy. 'I need some fish. I don't have any, and the shop can't give me any today. I didn't know what to do.'
Jim was really pleased. 'Do you want any chicken too?'
'Yes, I do.'
He sold all the fish and most of the chicken to the cook and then he went back to Polly.

~ ■ ~

Polly was pleased the fish was gone. It did not smell very nice in her kitchen.

'But what about everything else? The ketchup and the drinks?' she asked

'Tom's going to sell them in his supermarket.'

'Great.'

'Yes, I'm going to take everything to him today. Everything but – '

'Not everything? I don't want any of this rubbish in my kitchen.'

'Everything but the potatoes.' There were three bags of potatoes in one corner. 'He doesn't want them.'

Later, they watched TV. There was a programme on about food and the cook talked about wine.

'You can make wine from many different things,' he said. 'Fruit, flowers and even vegetables. You can make very nice orange wine and wine from apples too.'

Jim watched this and thought for a bit.

'We can make wine.'

'Wine?'

'Yes. Potato wine.'

'Is that going to be nice?'

'Oh, yes. He said it was OK just now on TV.'

'And then what will we do?'
'Sell it. We can go to different houses and sell it.'
'I think it's a stupid idea.'
'Don't worry, dear. It's going to be wonderful.'

~ ■ ~

The next morning, he went to the library and got out a book about wine. He bought some sugar and some bottles and corks.

'It looks easy,' he said. He was reading the book over lunch. 'I'm going to start this afternoon.'

He washed the potatoes and then he peeled one. It took a long time so he didn't peel any more. He just cut them into pieces and threw them into the bath. He was using the bath because it was so big. When he threw one potato in, Polly's shampoo fell in too, but he didn't worry too much. Then he put in lots of sugar and left it.

He came downstairs.

Polly was angry when she saw the bathroom.

'I can't have a bath. There are hundreds of potatoes in the bath. And it smells terrible, like old socks.'

'I'm sorry. It's only going to be for a week.'

'A week? I want a bath now. And also where's my shampoo?'

'I don't know, dear. You can go to your mother's house. You can use her bath and her shampoo.'

'But the *smell*.'

'It's OK. After a while, it goes away.'

'All right. But tomorrow I want a bath.'

'But where will I put the wine?'

'I don't know and I don't care.'

~ ■ ~

The next day, the smell was worse. Polly was very angry and Jim put the potatoes in a wheelbarrow. He wheeled it to his mother's house, but she didn't even open the door, the smell was so bad. Then he went to Tom; Tom told him to throw them away. Then he went back home.

'I don't know where to put them.'

'Not in the house.'

Then he had another good idea.

'Not in the house,' he said slowly.

'That's what I said,' Polly replied.

'OK, Polly.'

He went outside to his shed. He put the wheelbarrow inside.

A few days later, Polly noticed a strange smell.

'What is that smell?'

She called a plumber to look at the drains, but he didn't find anything. Then she cleaned everywhere in the house, but there was still the strange smell. Then she went out to the shed in the garden. That night Jim stayed outside, Polly was so angry.

The next day, he read his book about wine and made about two hundred bottles of potato wine. Then they waited.

One day, Tom came round.

'Jim, what about the bicycle?'

'Oh, the bicycle.'

Tom wanted the money or the bicycle. Jim had forgotten both.

'Don't worry, I have a wonderful idea, and I need the bicycle. I'm going to give you the money. Don't worry.'

After Tom went, Polly asked him about the idea.

'A bike-taxi,' he said proudly.

'What?'

'Ordinary taxis are no good in the traffic. But a ride on a bike is very quick.'

Polly laughed. 'You're crazy.'

'No, I'm just a good businessman.'

He bought an old chair and tied it to the back of the bike. Now someone could sit on it. He took it to the station. When the train came in, lots of people wanted taxis and there was a queue. But no-one tried the bike. 'Too dangerous,' or 'Too noisy,' or 'Too cold,' they said. One student did try the bike-taxi but when Jim stopped, he ran off and did not pay.

He didn't take any money that morning, but after lunch he saw a little old lady with a large bird-cage.

'Would you like a ride?'

'Yes, I would. I love bicycles. What a clever idea.'

With the bird-cage it was difficult, but Jim drove carefully. The woman lived outside the town in a small village. When they got to the village, the old lady said she lived at the top of the hill. It was a big hill and Jim was not very fit. As he cycled up, he got very hot. Nearly at the top, a dog ran in front of them. Jim stopped very quickly and the old lady fell off. She wasn't hurt but the bird-cage was completely broken. She didn't pay because of the bird-cage and so, on the first day of the bike-taxi, Jim took no money.

The next day, he decided not to try any more.

~ ■ ~

He checked the shed. The wine looked quite good. It was very clear and golden, but when he tasted it, it was not ready yet.

~ ■ ~

He took the bicycle back to Tom, but on the way he saw a woman with a small child.

'I need a bike like that. When I go shopping, I need a seat for my boy.'

'Oh, I don't want it any more, actually,' Jim said.

'OK. I'll buy it.'

Jim was really happy. He went to Tom and gave him his money back. And he still had some money left.

~ ■ ~

On the way home, he stopped at a television shop and watched a Punch and Judy Show. It looked great and at the end of the show, the man collected some money from the crowd.

At home, he told Polly about it. She looked worried. 'You're not going to start that, are you?'

'Well, no. I don't think so.'

But later he bought some wood and paint. He went out to the shed and began work.

A week later, he finished a Punch and Judy set. He took it to the main street and set it up. In a few minutes, there was a big crowd. Everyone laughed and Jim was really happy.

There was a dog in front of the Punch and Judy tent. He chewed the material of the tent and then he pulled it hard. The Punch and Judy tent fell over and everyone could see Jim. He was very embarrassed. Everyone laughed and to his surprise, they gave him some money.

'Great. Really funny,' they all said.

When he got home, Polly was amazed at the money. And Jim decided to do it again.

~ ■ ~

The next time, the dog was not there and there were no mistakes. He didn't take so much money. When he tried again, only a few people stopped. Hardly anyone gave him any money. But he carried on. The next time, there was only a man with a beard and a checked jacket.

When Jim finished, he clapped.

'That was great, really swell.' The man was American.

'Thank you.'

'You know, at home there is nothing like this.'

'Oh, really?'

'I love it. Can I buy it?'

'Well . . . '

'I know, you love it too. I just like it so much. I can give you a good price.'

'Well, perhaps . . . '

The American paid a lot of money for the Punch and Judy, and Jim was pleased. Polly was happy too.

'Sometimes you're quite clever.'

'I'm such a good businessman.'

~ ■ ~

Later that evening, there was a large bang like an explosion.

'What was that?' And they rushed into the garden. In the shed, one of the bottles of potato wine was broken.

'It exploded,' Jim said. 'It's ready.'

In the kitchen, they tested some.

'It's OK.' He started laughing. 'Quite strong.'

'It's not very nice, but it's strong. Very strong.' Polly started laughing.

'Let's go and sell some.'

They went to their neighbours and offered them some. Everybody agreed it was strong, but everyone bought a dozen bottles.

~ ■ ~

Back at home, they laughed.

'All this money from potatoes,' Polly said.

'It was a good idea. Shall we drink some more?'

'Yes, let's.'

They both laughed and laughed and laughed.

'Is there any more left?'

'About ten bottles. I'm going to make some more.'

'Good idea.'

Then the doorbell rang and
there was a policeman there.

'Have you been making wine?'

'Yes, do you want some?
It's very good.'

'No, sir. I don't.'

'Oh, but it's very nice. Well,
very strong . . . ' Jim said.

Polly laughed very loudly.
She was drunk.

'You can't sell wine, sir.'

'Why, everyone likes it.'

'No, sir.'

'But –'

'Don't sell any more. If you sell
any more, you're going to prison.'

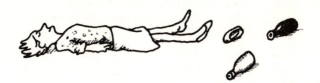

'Would you like to *try* some?'
Polly asked.
   'Well. No thank you, madam.'
   'A little. It's like juice, not like wine.'
   'Really? Well, OK. Just a little.
Selling juice is OK.'
   'It's OK.'
   He started laughing.
   'I'm going now.'
   And then he fell over.

~ ■ ~

Jim did not make any more wine. He decided to start
another business. Polly was worried. He had some strange
ideas nowadays.
   Tom met Jim that evening in the pub.
   'Have a drink?' said Jim.
   'No, I'm going to buy you one. A whisky?'

'Yes. Thank you.'
Tom got him the drink and sat down.
'Can you be my new manager?' Tom said.
'New manager?'
'Yes, I want someone with lots of ideas. I want you.'
Jim was very surprised.
'That's great. But – well, I have this idea.'
Tom laughed.
'Potato wine? No more ideas. Take the manager's job.'
'Well, perhaps you're right. I also have lots of ideas for your supermarket.'

Exercises

1 Why is Jim sad at the beginning of the story?

2 What happened when Jim got the train to London?

3 Where did Jim work in London?

4 Why did he go back home?

5 Why does Jim buy a bicycle?

6 Why is the business not a success?

7 What did Jim make with the potatoes?

8 Why was Polly angry?

9 What did Jim do with the bicycle?

10 Who bought his Punch and Judy show?

11 What happened when Jim and Polly drank the wine?

12 Who gives Jim a job at the end? Do you think he will be good at the job?

Glossary

27   *proudly* (adv):   feeling very happy with yourself
      ' 'A bike taxi,' he said proudly.'

29   ***Punch and Judy*** (n):   a traditional funny puppet
      show for children
      'On the way home, he stopped at a television shop
      and watched a Punch and Judy show.'

16   *sack* (n):   big bag
      ' 'I want some potatoes, Tony. Five sacks.' '

 4   *scream* (v):   make a very loud noise
      'She screamed and everyone looked at her.'

24   *shampoo* (n):   (bottle of liquid) for washing your
      hair
      'When he threw one potato in, Polly's shampoo
      fell in too, but he didn't worry too much.'

21   *stolen* (adj):   something you took that did not belong
      to you
      ' 'Why? Is it stolen?' '

30   *swell* (adj, Am Eng):   very good
      ' 'That was great, really swell.' '

 2   ***unemployment blackspot*** (n):   place where many
      people have no work
      'Today, the Prime Minister visited one of the
      country's unemployment blackspots: the North
      East.'

25   *wheelbarrow* (n):   a small cart used for carrying
      things, which has a wheel at the front and two legs at
      the back
      'Polly was very angry and Jim put the potatoes in
      a wheelbarrow.'

Language Grading in the **Macmillan Bookshelf Series**

This reader has been written using a loosely controlled range of language structures. There is no tight control of vocabulary as it is based on the authors' experience of the kind of vocabulary range expected at each particular language level. The authors have also taken care to contextualise any unfamiliar words, which are further explained in the glossary. We hope you will try to deduce meaning from the context, and will use a dictionary where necessary to expand your lexical knowledge.

The language items listed here show those most commonly used at each level in the **Bookshelf** series:

Level One (elementary)
Mainly simple and compound sentences, beginning to use more complex sentences but with limited use of sub clauses

Present Simple	Positive and negative statements
Present Continuous	Interrogative
(present and future reference)	Imperative
Past Continuous	And, or, but, so, because, before, after
'Going to' future	Some/any (-thing)
Past Simple	Basic adjectives
(regular and a few common irregular)	Some common adverbs
Can (ability)	'Simple' comparatives, superlatives
Would like (offer, request)	Gerunds/infinitives, common verbs

Level Two (lower intermediate)
Simple and compound sentences, limited use of complex sentences

Present Perfect	Conditional, can, could (possibility)
Will/won't future	When/while
Present/Past Simple Passive	Question tags, reflexives
Have to, must, should, could	Comparatives, superlatives
Can/may (requests/permission)	(common adjectives/adverbs)
Infinitives (like, want, try, etc.)	Reported speech (present/past)
Gerunds (start, finish, after, like, etc.)	

Level Three (intermediate)
More complex sentences, including embedded clauses

Present Perfect Continuous	Conditionals 1 and 2
Past Perfect	Although, to/in order to, since
Present/Past Continuous Passives	(reason)
Perfect Passives	So/neither
Ought to	Reported statements, requests, etc.
May/might (possibility)	

Level Four (upper intermediate)
At this stage there is minimal control, although authors generally avoid unnecessary complexity

Future Continuous	More complex passives
Past Perfect Continuous	Conditionals 3

Fish and Chips
and Other Adventures

Titles in this series: